SIMPLE PLEASURES

Nesting

CONARI PRESS

First published in 2004 by Conari Press,
an imprint of Red Wheel/Weiser, LLC
York Beach, ME
With offices at:
368 Congress Street
Boston, MA 02210
www.redwheelweiser.com

Adapted from the *Simple Pleasures* series first published in 1996 by Conari Press.

ISBN 1-57324-962-9

Printed in the United States
PC

11 10 09 08 07 06 05 04
 8 7 6 5 4 3 2 1

The paper used in this publication meets the minimum requirements of the
American National Standard for Information Sciences—Permanence of Paper for
Printed Library Materials Z39.48-1992 (R1997).

Nesting

*H*ome. I love being at home. In fact, it's hard to blast me out of the house. Looking back at my life as a whole now that I'm in my forties, I realized I was bitten young by the domestic bug.

My instincts for creating a comfortable nest and sitting in it contentedly have never left me. No matter what my circumstances have been—I've settled in with dozens of houseplants, tacked up a few pieces of artwork, and proceeded to needlepoint pillows, burn incense, and cook dinners from scratch every night. Even now, often I don't leave the house for days on end.

It's been through homemaking that I have experienced some of the greatest pleasures in my life. And so, once again, I asked people to share their stories, recipes, crafts, and other homespun creature comforts. *Simple Pleasures of Nesting* will help you to connect with the heart of your home, to what truly matters to you in your daily life.

6

$\mathcal{A}$ craft from Victorian times that seems to have gone out of favor is the making of memory plates. These are collages that are made from photos and other paper memorabilia and then attached to the back of a clear glass plate and displayed in the living room or study. They can be very beautiful, because the colors in whatever artwork you've chosen are seen through the glass, making it look as if the artwork is under water.

1 translucent glass plate
photos and images of your choice cut from magazines
   or catalogs
decoupage fixative (available at craft stores)
tissue paper
spray glue
polyurethane

Create the design you want on a similar-sized plate and then trans-
fer the images one at a time to the glass plate. Apply the decoupage
glue to the front of the image and then press the image onto the
back of the plate, carefully pressing out any bubbles or wrinkles.
When your design is complete, cut out a piece of tissue paper the
same size as the plate and glue it to the back of the images, so that
from behind you will see only a white surface. Seal the back and the
rim of the plate with 3 coats of polyurethane, allowing it to dry completely between coats.

HANDMADE PRETZELS

Pretzels are great nonfat snacks that can easily be made at home. The longer you knead the dough, the softer the pretzel will be. If you've got kids, enlist them—to make the process more fun, the dough can easily be formed in the shapes of letters and numbers.

1 ½ cups warm water
1 package yeast
1 tablespoon sugar

4 cups flour
1 teaspoon salt, plus more for tops
1 egg, beaten

Preheat oven to 425°. Put the warm water into a large bowl, sprinkle in yeast, and stir until it dissolves. Add sugar, flour, and salt. Mix well, then knead dough until it is smooth and soft. Roll and twist dough into desired shapes—letters, numbers, twists, and so on. Grease two cookie sheets. Lay the pretzel dough shapes onto cookie sheets. Brush with beaten egg and sprinkle lightly with salt. Bake for 12 to 15 minutes, or until golden. Makes 1 to 2 dozen, depending on size.

BASKET OF LOVE

Do you want to surprise your paramour some evening? Make a love basket. Simply find a heart-shaped basket, spray-paint it red (sand it slightly first so the paint will stick better), add a pretty ribbon to the handle, and fill it with your beloved's favorite things: chocolate-covered cherries, sexy underwear— whatever he or she fancies. Then place it on your love's pillow to be discovered.

*I*n her reminiscence with recipes, *We Called It Macaroni* (Alfred A. Knopf, 1996), Nancy Verde Barr recalls that "pasta fazool" didn't seem like much of a treat when she was growing up. But when she was pregnant with her first child, she began to crave this comforting soup, and made many a mad dash to Italian restaurants in Providence, Rhode Island, for a container of hot, soothing soup to go. Here's one version, although as with most comfort food, there are dozens of equally tasty variations.

continued

PASTA E FAGIOLI

1 cup dried white or cranberry beans, or 2 ½ cups
    canned beans, drained and rinsed
¼ pound bacon, chopped or 2 ounces pancetta, minced
2 tablespoons olive oil (if using pancetta)
1 onion, finely chopped
1 rib celery, finely chopped
1 carrot, peeled and finely chopped
2 cloves garlic, minced
2–4 tomatoes, peeled and chopped
salt and fresh ground pepper
¼ pound small, tubular macaroni or noodles
Parmesan or pecorino cheese

If using dried beans, soak overnight in water, drain, cover again with
water and simmer for about 2 hours, or until beans are tender. Set
aside.

In a large saucepan, fry bacon until barely crisp or saute pancetta in olive oil about 4 minutes, until fat is rendered. Drain off most of fat.

Add the onion, celery, carrot, and garlic, and saute gently about 10 minutes, until vegetables are soft.

If using canned beans, heat in 4 cups water or meat broth. If using dried beans, reheat in a large pot. Add bacon vegetable mixture and tomatoes to beans, return to a simmer, add macaroni or noodles and cook until pasta is tender. Serve warm with freshly ground pepper and grated Parmesan or pecorino cheese. Serves 6.

*B*ecause so many of us work primarily with our heads, doing something with our hands can be tremendously satisfying. I have an old pine blanket chest that I bought about twenty years ago. Over the years it has endured dog scratches, children's scribbles, and scrapes from candleholders. One day I decided it needed some help. So I sanded it down a bit and applied coat after coat of Briwax and then cream furniture polish. Now it glows again, and I smile every time I walk into the room. Find something with intrinsic quality and value. If someone once cared about the piece, no matter how many layers of paint and neglect it has endured, you can restore it. Enjoy your creativity and a sense of preserving the past. Or do what my co-worker Brenda does. Find a junky wooden or metal chair that is being thrown away and save it from the landfill. Use your imagination and paint it to have a one-of-a-kind creation. Each leg a different color? The sky on the seat? Let your imagination soar.

NOSTALGIC BROWNIES

2 ounces unsweetened
   chocolate
¼ cup butter
1 cup sugar
1 egg

1 teaspoon vanilla
½ cup all-purpose flour
pinch of salt
½ cup walnuts, broken into
   pieces or chopped

Preheat the oven to 300 degrees. Butter an 8-inch square baking pan, and line it with baking parchment or waxed paper. Butter and flour the waxed paper.

Melt the chocolate and butter in a saucepan over low heat. Remove from heat, stir well, then lightly stir in the sugar, egg, vanilla, flour, salt, and nuts.

Spread into the pan and bake for about 30 minutes, until center is set. Do not overbake, or brownies will lose their chewy texture and become dry.

Remove pan from the oven and cool on a rack about 5 minutes. Turn out onto the rack and peel off the paper. While still warm, cut into squares with a greased knife. Makes 16 brownies.

$\mathcal{M}$aking pressed flowers is incredibly easy. It requires no special equipment and costs absolutely nothing. Here's how: When your new telephone book comes, save the old one and put it somewhere where you won't lose it. Find a meadow and collect small bouquets of wildflowers. Lay them flat in different parts of the phone book. Place a small boulder, or anything else that's heavy and not likely to take off, on top of the phone book. Let sit for a few months.

18

*P*lace pressed flowers in a pattern you like on the front of blank cards or on stiff artists' paper you can get at a craft or variety store. Attach them to the paper with a dab of glue. Peel an appropriate amount of transparent, self-stick plastic film (like contact paper) from the roll and carefully place on top of the flowers, pressing from the center to the edge to eliminate air bubbles. Trim the edge of the plastic to match the card or paper. You can then send them to your friends for Christmas, birthdays, Valentine's Day, or no reason at all. Bookmarks can be made in exactly the same way—just cut the paper to an appropriate size.

19

FABRIC-COVERED LAMP SHADE

If you would rather make a shade from a kit and are having trouble finding what you want, contact The Lamp Shop in New Hampshire (603-224-1603) or Wisconsin Lighting in Wisconsin (715-834-8707).

1 plain, white, unpleated, translucent shade
brown paper
spray glue or fabric glue
about 1 yard lightweight or medium-weight fabric
    (length depends on size of shade)

First make a pattern by wrapping the brown paper around the shade and taping it in place. Crimp the top and bottom to mark the edges and cut excess.

Remove the paper and trace the pattern on the wrong side of fabric, adding 1 inch to all sides for overlap. Cut out fabric.

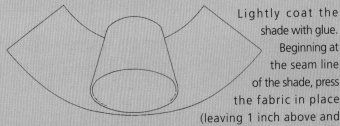

Lightly coat the shade with glue. Beginning at the seam line of the shade, press the fabric in place (leaving 1 inch above and below the top and bottom of shade). Carefully wrap the fabric around the shade, smoothing out wrinkles or air bubbles as you go. When you reach the seam line again, fold the end of the fabric under a half-inch and overlap the beginning end, covering it completely. Glue in place. At the top and bottom, clip the fabric every inch or so, then fold down and glue these flaps to the inside.

NATURALLY DYED EASTER EGGS

Want to do something a little more sophisticated this Easter? You and your older kids might enjoy the subtle beauty of these natural wonders. But be aware—these are for decoration only. Do not eat.

1 red cabbage
3 very large brown-skinned onions
1 dozen eggs
36 rubber bands
2 dozen small fern fronds and/or fresh and dried flower blossoms
1 tablespoon powdered alum
1 roll cheesecloth

Without cutting the cabbage in two, cut the central core out and separate the leaves so that each leaf is as large as possible. Cut the two ends off the onions and peel the skin off, again keeping each piece of skin as large as possible.

Place a fern or flower against an egg on either side and wrap it completely with a red cabbage leaf, using two rubber bands to keep it on. Repeat for five more eggs. Use the onion skins and remaining flowers and ferns for the other six eggs, again using two rubber bands to affix. Cut 12 pieces of cheesecloth big enough to wrap completely around each egg and secure with two more rubber bands.

Place the cabbage eggs in one pot and the onion eggs in another. Add water and 1 ½ teaspoon alum to each pot. Bring to a boil, reduce heat, and simmer for 15 minutes. Remove from heat and allow eggs to cool in water. Unwrap and enjoy your designs. Makes 1 dozen.

SIMPLE PLEASURES

PERSONALIZED REFRIGERATOR MAGNETS

Can you ever have enough kitchen magnets? With all the stuff I tack up on my fridge, I certainly can't. Here's an easy way to make your own (and they're great gifts for Grandma that kids can make by themselves.)

Save the metal lids from frozen drink cans.

Find some favorite photos that will fit on the lids, and have color copies made of them.

Cut the copies to fit, and using white glue or spray glue, affix the pictures to the lids, smoothing out any bubbles or wrinkles with your fingers.

Glue a thin piece of ribbing around the edge and a magnet on the back. Presto!

THE ZEN OF VACUUMING

SIMPLE PLEASURES

I never wear shoes unless I have to. I always go barefoot if I'm painting or cooking. I like to feel the ground against my skin, with no interruption in the energy that comes through my feet. I prefer to live in the desert, where I don't need shoes either inside or outside. And wherever I'm living, clean floors are essential.

My love affair with vacuuming began when I was a child. The noise blocked out my mother's scolding, and I could feel like I was doing something that made grownups proud of me. Vacuuming is still my joy and meditation. I totally check out when I'm running my Electrolux over the floor. Sometimes I go over the same spot over and over again. I feel about my Electrolux the way some people feel about classic cars. It's like an old DeSoto or Studebaker. It never gets too old, it just keeps getting more stylish, and it gets the job done. The only thing better than walking barefoot on a freshly vacuumed floor is getting a foot massage.

PERSONALIZED FURNITURE

We don't have a lot of money. So when I was pregnant, my husband and I hit all the garage sales looking for nursery items. We found an old chest of drawers for $20 and painted it white. When the baby was born, we dipped her hands and feet in water-based, latex pastel paints and then gently stamped her hand- and footprints on the top and sides of the dresser. Now we have a permanent reminder of her babyhood that she, and we, will treasure always.

LEMON BEESWAX POLISH

For those who love the glow of freshly polished wood furniture, here's a real treat—homemade furniture polish. Nothing beats the smell of lemon and beeswax!

⅔ cup boiling water
1 tablespoon liquid lemon dish detergent
2 ounces beeswax
½ ounce paraffin
1 ¼ cups turpentine
10 drops lemon essential oil
wide-neck jar with lid

Pour the boiling water into the dish detergent and allow to cool. In a double boiler, heat beeswax, paraffin, and turpentine over very low heat, taking care that mixture doesn't get hot enough to flare up. Whisk soap water into wax to form an emulsion. Add essential oil. Store in a wide-neck jar with a lid. Makes about 2 cups.

SLEEP POTION

Here is a marvelous aromatherapy spray from Judith Fitzsimmons' and Paula M. Bousquet's wonderful book *Seasons of Aromatherapy*. Guaranteed to relax you and help you drift off.

2 drops chamomile essential oil
4 drops lavender essential oil
3 drops orange essential oil
5 ounces water

Mix all ingredients together in a spray bottle. Spray bed clothing and the air before bedtime.

I grew up in a part of the South where it was often so hot and muggy on summer nights that my sisters and I couldn't get to sleep. Finally my parents came up with a solution to the problem. They told us we could each put one sheet in the fridge at supper. By bedtime the sheet would be crisp and cold, and when I crawled under it, the cool cotton draped over my skin was utterly calming. First I'd lie on the left side, and when that part of the sheet warmed up, I'd simply slide over one body width to where it was still cool. The sheet was exactly four body widths wide, but I was usually asleep before I used them all up. It felt so good I got to looking forward to going to bed, and sticky summer nights became a pleasure instead of an irritation.

31

High on the list of universal comfort

foods is potatoes. And when you are talking a real fall treat, there is nothing to compare to garlic and potatoes together. Is it possible that no one combined mashed potatoes and garlic before "garlic mashed potatoes" appeared on trendy restaurant menus and food magazine covers in the 1990s? We think not. The ancient bulb that the Chinese were praising in 3000 B.C. and the tuber that Spanish conquistadors discovered in Peru in the 16th century A.D. were surely meant for each other—two great underground resources merged into creamy bliss.

You can, if you like, simply toss peeled garlic cloves into the water when you boil potatoes and mash them together. But for a little more elegance, simmer the garlic in milk and cream while the potatoes cook. It will all come together perfectly.

continued

1 ½ pounds russet (baking) potatoes
8–10 cloves garlic
½ cup milk
½ cup cream
4–6 tablespoons butter
Salt and freshly ground black pepper to taste

Peel the potatoes, cut in half if large, cover with salted water and boil until tender, about 20 minutes. Drain, return to pot and shake until water is evaporated.

Meanwhile, peel garlic and slice in half lengthwise. If there is a green sprout in the center of the clove, lift it out and discard. Place garlic cloves, milk and cream in a small saucepan. Bring to a boil and cook, at lowest possible simmer, until garlic is tender, about 20 minutes. Remove the garlic with a fork or slotted spoon. Put the potatoes and garlic together through a ricer or food mill, if possible. Using an old-fashioned potato masher, mash potatoes and garlic together in a large bowl, adding butter, then milk and cream mixture, a little at a time, until desired consistency is reached. Add a little of the water in which the potatoes were boiled if needed.

Season with salt and pepper to taste. Serves 4.

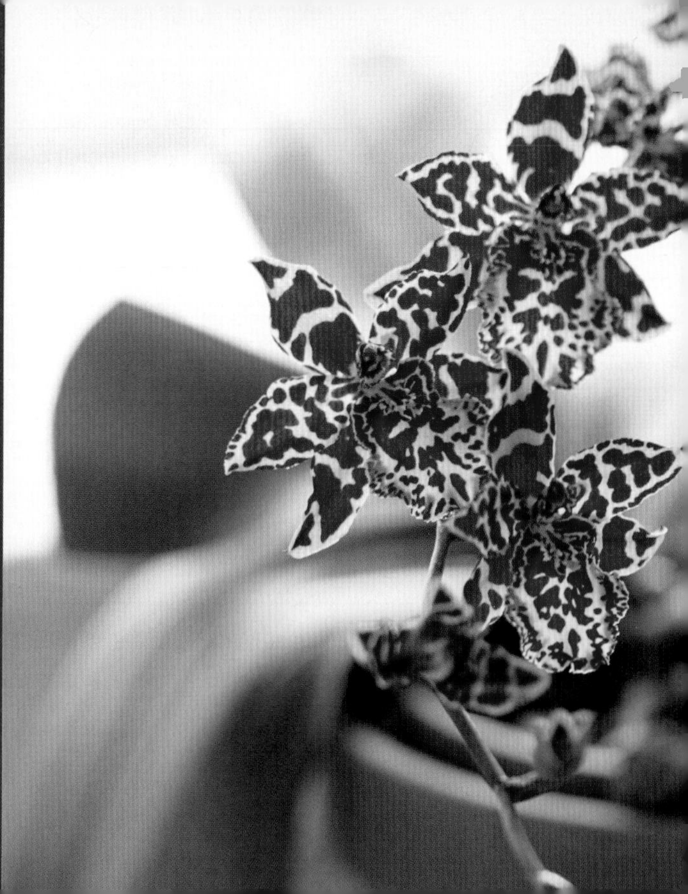

In the winter when my garden is dry and bare, nothing gives me more pleasure than to visit the local garden shop, where it always feels like sweet, balmy summer. I wander through the rows of brightly colored flowers and richly hued shiny leaves, and the aroma of blossoms and sweet rich earth make me forget, for a time, the gloom and doom outside. The plants and flowers are completely oblivious to the weather outside, and their verdant outbursts of energy restore mine. I take an inordinate amount of time picking out some ridiculously expensive and riotously colored plant that just screams warm weather, which I take home and place on my windowsill or bedside table in a beautiful basket or brightly colored cachepot. I kind of have a "brown thumb," so my plants never last long, but I almost prefer that; it gives me a chance to go to the garden shop again that much sooner!

THE KINDNESS BOX

*D*uring the weeks leading up to the holidays, we keep a kindness box. We wrap up a shoebox like a present and cut a slot in the top. Then we put the box and a pencil and some paper under the tree. When someone in the family notices someone doing something kind, we write the act down on a piece of paper and put it in the box. (Young children could draw a picture or tell Mom what they saw and ask her to write it down.) On Christmas Eve, along with reading a beautiful picture book of the Christmas story, we open the box and read all the notes.

The kiss of sun for pardon,
The song of the birds for mirth—
One is nearer God's Heart in a garden
Than anywhere else on earth.

—Dorothy Gurney

Rosemary is very good for hair, particularly dark hair, to which it imparts a wonderful shine. It will also help cut down on the problem of flyaway hair. This recipe makes enough for several applications.

8 drops cedar essential oil
8 drops lavender essential oil
12 drops rosemary essential oil
2 tablespoons olive oil

In a small glass container, mix the essential oils together. Add the olive oil. Pour about a teaspoon into the palm of your hand and rub hands together. Massage your head, hair, and scalp with the blend. Put a shower cap or warm towel on your head and leave it on for fifteen minutes. Wash and rinse your hair twice.

FAMILY HOME EVENING

*A*t one point I grew tired of running all over with all the kids every day—to soccer practice, games, piano lessons, tennis, play dates with friends. . . the list went on and on. I was exhausted, and the kids seemed cranky; there was never any downtime. It seemed as if we never had an evening to spend together as a family. Then I read about the tradition that Mormons have of a weekly "family home evening" and decided that was just what our family needed. And so I decreed Wednesdays as our home evening. After dinner, all of us spend the evening together with the TV off and with no outsiders, meetings, classes, or other commitments. Sometimes we play cards or a board game, read a story aloud, or tell ghost stories; other times we bake cookies together or just read in the same room. The kids protested at first, but now they too have gotten into the spirit.

43

The hours when the mind is
absorbed by beauty are the
only hours when we really
live...

—Richard Jefferies

Candles add a magical element

to any room. I especially love using the floating ones as a centerpiece for the dining room table, solving the problem of having an arrangement that interferes with conversation. Simply float a few candles and some flowers in a bowl, and you have an elegant focal point.

12 ounces paraffin
60 drops your favorite essential oil
12 1-inch floating candlewicks (available at craft
    stores)
12 metal pastry tins or candle molds

In a double boiler, melt the paraffin and then add the essential oil with a wooden spoon. Pour wax into molds slowly to avoid air bubbles. Let half set and then insert wicks in the center of each. Let candles set fully and then unmold. Makes 1 dozen.

*T*here are a number of wonderful ways to display photos inexpensively. Here are some ideas to get you started:

- To make photo collages, collect different-sized pictures in frames from yard sales and flea markets. Throw the pictures away. Cut a poster board the size of the frame for the backdrop, then create a collage with snapshots, gluing the pictures to the poster board, and insert into the frame. Think in themes—birthdays, holidays over the years, your daughter's volleyball career, vacation shots of you and your husband.

- Purchase inexpensive clear 8-by-10-inch acrylic box frames and have favorite photos blown up to 8-by-10-inch. Arrange them attractively on the wall.

- Find old window frames without glass. Tack pictures and other mementos on the wall and place the frames over them to create the illusion of looking through a window.

This is a fun project, especially for kids. But be sure to crack the eggs outside!

- raw eggs
- fingernail scissors
- confetti

Do this over a large bowl. With the fingernail scissors, cut a small hole at one end of the egg and a larger hole, about the size of a nickel, at the other. Clean out the egg by blowing into the small hole and allowing the insides to come out the large hole into the bowl. (Later make some scrambled eggs!) Rinse each shell carefully with water and allow to dry. Fill the egg with confetti through the large hole, then tape up the holes until ready to use. Crack them over an unsuspecting person, and watch his or her reaction.

HANDMADE PIÑATA

When I moved to California, I discovered that birthday parties for kids always included a piñata. Available at Mexican markets or party supply stores, they're great for kids under ten. But you can easily construct your own (kids can help)—and you don't need to wait for a birthday.

Get a very large balloon and blow it up.

Cut up newspaper into ½-inch strips. Dip each strip into a bowl of undiluted laundry starch. Then wrap the strip around the balloon. Continue until the balloon is completely covered.

Allow to dry completely, then paint with poster paint and cut a hole in the top (the balloon will pop; that's okay) to drop the treats in it. On either side of the big hole, cut a small hole and insert a strong cord for the hanger.

Fill the balloon with candy, small gifts, nuts, and so on. (If you like, you can turn your piñata into a bird by adding construction paper head and wings, and crepe-paper feathers.)

Suspend with a rope and pulley so you can raise and lower it while blindfolded adults and children take turns whacking it with a stick. When someone breaks it open, everyone scrambles for the goodies.

DRIED FLOWER DECORATIONS

Anyone who has ever had a Christmas tree has probably made paper, popcorn, or cranberry chains and perhaps even more elaborate handmade ornaments.

One simple and elegant way to decorate a Christmas tree is with small bunches of dried flowers. They are very easy to make and, if stored carefully—don't crush—will last year after year. You can use almost any dried flowers, but try a combination of lavender, fresh rosemary, baby's breath, roses, and statice.

First cut each flower into small sprigs and place in separate piles. Lay two or three sprigs of rosemary on the table. Add a sprig of baby's breath, then a few roses and statice. Tie the stems together with florists' wire (leaving a length of wire long enough to attach the spray to the tree), so that the stems are tight and the flowers fan out at the top. If you want a scent, sprinkle a few drops of an essential oil. These can also be used to decorate mirrors, picture frames, or place settings.

So named because I love to use
this herbal combination.

LOVE BATH

1 cup dried lavender
1 cup dried rosemary
1 cup dried rose petals
½ cup dried lovage
½ cup dried lemon verbena
¼ cup each dried thyme, mint, sage, and orris root
muslin

55

Mix all dried herbs together and store in a covered container. When
you want to take a bath, place ¼ cup of herbal mix in the center of
an 8-inch square of muslin and tie tightly with a piece of string. Boil
this ball in 1 quart of water for 10 minutes. Draw a warm bath, pour
in the herbal water, and use the ball to scrub your body. Makes 16
bath balls.

FABULOUS FOOT RUB

*I*f a foot rub is your idea of a good time, try doing one with peppermint foot lotion. Many people swear by it as the only curative after a long walk or a hard day of work (or of shopping!). The Body Shop sells a superior foot lotion. You can also make your own by adding 1 tablespoon of peppermint oil to 6 ounces of unscented lotion. Or try this therapeutic indulgence, courtesy of the Fredericksburg Herb Farm in Fredericksburg, Texas: grate approximately 1 cup of fresh ginger. Squeeze gently and add, along with a few drops of olive oil, to a foot basin or tub filled with hot water. Cover the bowl with a cloth or towel to preserve the heat, and soak for fifteen minutes. Then dry your feet and slip into a pair of warm socks.

57

You can easily make your own flavored olive oils. Buy some decorative bottles or use recycled wine bottles. Be sure to use only fresh herbs, to wash them well, to make sure the oil completely covers all the ingredients, and to seal the bottle tightly and use within three weeks. Because garlic contains the spores for a bacteria that, when added to oil, can cause botulism, it's best not to make any garlic-flavored oil (the store-bought kind uses sterilized garlic).

58

To make chili oil, simply add 5 yellow Thai chilies and 1 teaspoon peppercorns to 5 cups of olive oil, cap the bottle tightly, and let stand in a cool place for a week.

For lemon pepper oil, slice a lemon for each bottle you plan to make and dry in oven at 170° for about 5 hours, or until dry but not crisp. To a bottle of oil, add 1 tablespoon whole black peppercorns and the slices from one dried lemon.

For rosemary oil, add 3 large sprigs of rosemary to a bottle of olive oil.

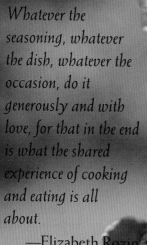

Whatever the seasoning, whatever the dish, whatever the occasion, do it generously and with love, for that in the end is what the shared experience of cooking and eating is all about.

—Elizabeth Rozin

HOMEMADE VANILLA EXTRACT

Yes, you can do it, and it is unbelievably easy. If you place it in a pretty glass bottle, it makes a lovely little gift.

   1 vanilla bean
   1 4-ounce bottle with top
   scant 4 ounces vodka

Split the bean in half, put in the bottle, and pour in the vodka. Cap and let sit at least one month. (The longer, the stronger.)

WINTER STEW

A satisfying and simple light supper. Just omit the sausage and you have a vegetarian entree. Can be served over rice.

2 tablespoons olive oil
¼ cup green or pepper
1 cup chopped onion
4 cloves chopped garlic
2 cups chopped fresh spinach
2 cups chopped cabbage
1 14 ½-ounce can tomatoes

1 cup frozen lima beans
4 ounces fully cooked sausage, such as andouille (for a spicier stew) or kielbasa, sliced
¼ cup chopped parsley
2 14 ½-ounce cans of beef, chicken, or vegetable broth

In a large pot, heat the olive oil over medium-high heat and add green pepper, onion, and garlic. Saute until vegetables are tender, about 5 minutes. Add the remaining ingredients and simmer until cabbage is cooked, about 10 minutes. Serves 4.

To be simple is to be great.
—Ralph Waldo Emerson